When Your Dad Was Little

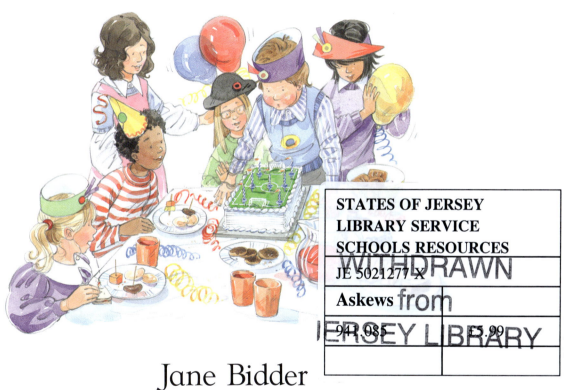

Jane Bidder

Illustrated by Shelagh McNicholas

W
FRANKLIN WATTS
LONDON•SYDNEY

For my husband Bill
and all dads everywhere − J.B.

For Liam, James and Joe − S.M.

The author and publisher would like to thank everyone who contributed memories to this book.

This edition 2007
First published in 2004 by Franklin Watts
338 Euston Road, London NW1 3BH

Franklin Watts Australia
Level 17/207 Kent Street, Sydeny, NSW 2000

Text © Jane Bidder 2004
Illustrations © Franklin Watts 2004

Editor: Caryn Jenner
Visualiser: James Marks
Art director: Jonathan Hair
Picture research: Diana Morris
Photography: Ray Moller unless otherwise credited.

Picture credits: Bettmann/Corbis: 7, 28t. Corbis: 18c. Bob Daemmrich/Image Works/Topham: 6, 28b.
Hulton Archive: front cover tl, 9b, 12c. © IPC Magazines: 24b. NASA: 15t. Topham: 10t.

Every attempt has been made to clear copyright. Should there be any inadvertent omission
please apply to the publisher for rectification.

A CIP catalogue record for this book is available from the British Library.

ISBN 978-0-7496-7815-9

Printed in China

Franklin Watts is a division of Hachette Children's Books, an Hachette Livre UK Company.

Contents

Changing times

These pictures show children in the present and in the past.

You are growing up in the present.

Present
This is a picture of children in the present. ▼

◀ **Past**
This is a picture of children in the past. This picture was taken in 1977.

Your dad grew up in the past. Many things have changed since your dad was a child.

In this book, lots of different fathers remember what it was like when they were your age.

Go-kart

"When I was little, my dad and I made a go-kart with old things from the shed. I used to go really fast in my go-kart and pretend I was a racing car driver!"

This go-kart was made with parts from an old pram.

School desks

"When I was little, my desk at school had a lift-up lid. I put my books and things inside my desk and pictures of my favourite football players under the lid."

The teachers wrote on a chalkboard. The chalk made a squeaking noise on the board!

Dr Who

"When I was little, my friend and I used to pretend we were Daleks. They were the robots in *Dr Who*, our favourite TV show. We thought the Daleks were very scary!"

Dr Who travelled through time to save the world from the Daleks. The show first came on TV in 1963.

Moon walk

"When I was little, I watched the first Moon walk on TV. It was amazing! I told my dad that I wanted to go to the Moon, too."

In 1969, Americans Neil Armstrong and Edwin Aldrin became the first people on the Moon.

Grandma's garden

"When I was little, I lived in China. I loved to visit my grandma in the countryside. I used to pick guava fruits from the tree in her garden. Grandma also had pigs in her garden, and they liked guavas, too!"

Guava trees grow in warm places. The fruit is sweet and juicy.

Slide shows

"When I was little, my friends used to come over to my house for a slide show. The slide projector shone the pictures on the wall. We felt like we had our own cinema!"

The slides were shown one picture at a time. There was no sound, but children often made up stories to go with the pictures.

Old money

"When I was little, we used old coins like shillings and sixpence. Then we changed to the new money that we have now. It was hard to work out how much to pay at the sweet shop!"

These are old coins. In 1971, people in Britain began using new money.

Bughari bread

"When I was little, I lived in Africa. I used to help my mum make bughari bread with a plant called manioc. I shaped the bread dough into little loaves, then my mum cooked it in the pot."

To make the bread, you have to grind the manioc into flour. Manioc is also called cassava. The bread has different names.

Comic books

"When I was little, I loved to read comic books. Every Thursday, I got *Whizzer and Chips* delivered to my house. My friend got *Look and Learn*. We used to share our comics so it was like having two for one."

The comics had lots of funny stories. Some comics also had puzzles and competitions.

My birthday

"When I was little, my birthday was the best day of the year. Everyone sang 'Happy Birthday', then I blew out the candles on my cake. I felt so special. Now that I'm a dad, I like to make birthdays special for my own son."

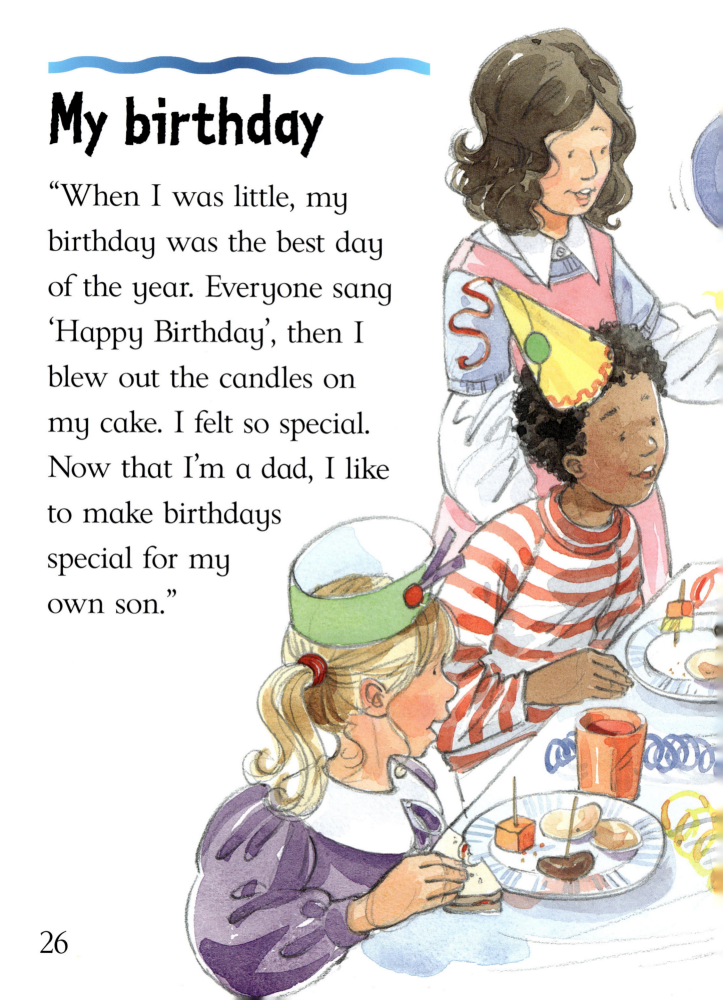

Timeline

This timeline shows the years from 1960 to 2010.

1960

1970

1980

During the 1980s and 1990s, these dads were young grown-ups.

1990

2000

2010

During the 1960s and 1970s, the dads in this book were children.

You are a child now. What year were you born? When do you think you will be grown up?

Memories

Ask your dad about when he was a child. Ask your teachers and other grown-ups about their memories, too. Here are some questions to ask.

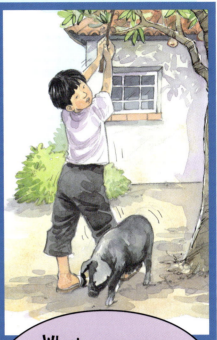

How was your school different from mine?

What were your favourite toys and games?

What kinds of clothes did you wear?

What things do we have now that you didn't have when you were a child?

What special events do you remember?

Glossary

Memories   Things you remember from the past. Do you *memories* of your last birthday?

Remember   To think of the past. Do you *remember* what you did yesterday?

Past   Time gone by. The *past* can mean yesterday or it can mean a long time ago. Your dad was a child in the *past*.

Present   Now. Today is in the *present*. You are a child in the *present*.

Timeline   A chart that shows the passing of time. See the *timeline* on page 28.

Index